INTRODUCTION

In the dynamic sphere of contemporary business, where strategic networking serves as the linchpin to success, LinkedIn emerges as the digital nexus of professional connectivity. Imagine a seasoned business leader seated amidst the pulse of industry innovation and the cadence of ambitious objectives. Confronted with the universal query of leveraging LinkedIn to augment her business trajectory, our protagonist, an astute entrepreneur, delves into the uncharted territories of LinkedIn Sales Navigator.

LinkedIn Sales Navigator, a formidable ally in the pursuit of business excellence, transcends the conventional boundaries of virtual networking. As our protagonist navigates the intricate landscape of this robust tool, she encounters a transformative experience. Advanced search filters become not just tools but instruments of precision, guiding her towards prospective clients, fostering strategic alliances, and uncovering unexplored market segments.

This book, "LinkedIn Sales Navigator: The Completely New Advanced LinkedIn Search Filters Guide for Business Growth on LinkedIn," isn't merely a handbook; it's an educational expedition into the nuanced realm of digital networking. Whether you're a seasoned executive or a burgeoning entrepreneur, the insights embedded within these pages are designed to recalibrate your approach to LinkedIn, elevating it beyond a mere platform to a catalyst for profound business transformation.

Embark on a systematic exploration of advanced search filters, where each strategic click propels you closer to your organizational objectives. Within these chapters, discover methodologies employed by industry leaders who have harnessed the full potential of LinkedIn Sales Navigator, charting new trajectories for their enterprises.

Are you prepared to revolutionize your business strategy through the lens of LinkedIn Sales Navigator? This expedition commences here, offering LinkedIn Sales Navigator not just as a tool but as an indispensable guide to redefining your path to business growth.

BEFORE YOU GO,

Emerging Trends In Social Selling

In the boundless realm of professional networking and business growth, the art of social selling is undergoing a profound transformation. As we embark on this journey into the heart of LinkedIn Sales Navigator, it is imperative to cast our gaze forward, recognizing the evolving landscape that will define the future of social selling.

As we set forth into the pages of this guide, let us not only explore the current landscape of social selling but also anticipate the horizons of tomorrow. The emerging trends discussed herein are not distant possibilities; they are the building blocks of the future of social selling. So, with anticipation in our hearts and innovation in our minds, let us embark on this journey together, where every connection has the potential to shape the landscape of social commerce.

Personalization Revolution:

The age of generic outreach is waning, making room for a new era of hyper-personalization. Social sellers are harnessing advanced tools and technologies to tailor their approaches, ensuring each interaction feels bespoke and resonates with the unique needs of the prospect.

Visual Storytelling Mastery:

Beyond words, the power of visual storytelling is taking center stage. As attention spans shorten, social sellers are adeptly incorporating videos, infographics, and compelling imagery to convey messages with impact, forging stronger connections through the art of visual communication.

Artificial Intelligence Unleashed:

The rise of artificial intelligence is not a distant horizon; it is here, shaping the way social sellers operate. From predictive analytics that anticipate buyer behavior to AI-driven insights guiding decision-making, the integration of intelligent technologies is becoming an indispensable ally in the social selling arsenal.

Seamless Social Commerce Integration:

The boundaries between social media and commerce are blurring. Social sellers are no longer just fostering connections; they are guiding prospects seamlessly through the entire buyer's journey, with social commerce features turning engagement into transactions within the social ecosystem.

Virtual Reality Networking Odyssey:

Imagine a world where networking transcends physical constraints. The realm of virtual reality (VR) and augmented reality (AR) is on the horizon, offering social sellers the opportunity to engage in immersive experiences, revolutionizing how relationships are forged and business is conducted.

Purpose-Driven Narratives:

Beyond products and services, social selling is embracing purpose-driven narratives. Successful social sellers are aligning their stories with values, weaving a tapestry of authenticity and meaning that resonates with an audience increasingly drawn to businesses with a sense of purpose.

Orchestrated Multi-Channel Symphony:

Social selling is no longer a solo performance on a single platform. Savvy practitioners are orchestrating their strategies across multiple channels, ensuring a harmonious and synchronized approach that amplifies their reach and impact.

Dynamic Content Ecosystem:

Content is evolving from static to dynamic. Social sellers are exploring interactive formats, dynamic content experiences, and engaging materials that invite participation, transforming the passive audience into active collaborators in the storytelling process.

Hyper-Personalized Journey Mapping:

The journey of a prospect is no longer a linear path. Social sellers are embracing data analytics and AI to craft hyper-personalized customer journeys, mapping every touchpoint with precision to create an experience tailored to the unique needs and preferences of each individual buyer.

Evolution of Social Platforms:

Social media platforms are living organisms, constantly evolving. Social sellers must not only adapt but anticipate these changes, staying at the forefront of emerging tools and features within platforms like LinkedIn Sales Navigator for sustained success in the dynamic world of social commerce.

Adapting To Technological Changes

In the ever-evolving tapestry of business and technology, adaptation is the compass that guides us through uncharted territories. It is crucial to first acknowledge the dynamic landscape that technological advancements have shaped as we stand on the verge of a thorough investigation into the complexities of LinkedIn Sales Navigator.

As we embark on this exploration into the realms of LinkedIn Sales Navigator, let us carry with us the recognition that adaptation is not a one-time event but a continuous journey. The pages ahead will unfold the intricacies of adapting to technological changes in the realm of professional networking and business growth, where every adaptation propels us toward new horizons.

Accelerated Technological Evolution:

The speed at which technology is advancing is unparalleled. From artificial intelligence to data analytics, the tools available to professionals are evolving at an accelerated pace. Adapting to these changes is not merely a choice but an imperative for those navigating the digital frontier.

Shaping Professional Landscapes:

Technological innovations are reshaping the very fabric of how professionals connect, engage, and transact. The advent of platforms like LinkedIn Sales Navigator is not just a feature; it is a reflection of the transformative impact technology has on our approach to networking, sales, and business development.

The Imperative of Continuous Learning:

In a landscape where algorithms update and interfaces transform, the commitment to continuous learning becomes a linchpin. Social sellers and business professionals must be agile learners, ready to assimilate new tools and methodologies to remain at the forefront of their industries.

Integration of Artificial Intelligence:

The infusion of artificial intelligence is not a distant vision —it is the present reality. Machines are becoming adept at analyzing data, predicting trends, and offering insights. Adapting to this shift means harnessing the power of AI as a collaborator, allowing it to augment our capabilities.

Data-Driven Decision Making:

Data is no longer just information; it is the cornerstone of strategic decision-making. Professionals must transition from gut-based decisions to data-driven insights. With its analytics and metrics, LinkedIn Sales Navigator is a prime example of the age in which concrete, real-time data informs decisions.

Transformative Impact on Networking:

Networking, once confined to physical events, has transcended traditional boundaries. Technological changes have democratized access to networks, allowing professionals to forge connections, nurture relationships, and conduct business on a global scale. Adaptation means embracing the expansive reach that technology affords.

The Rise of Virtual Collaboration:

The digital realm has given rise to virtual collaboration. Teams no longer need to be co-located to work cohesively. Adapting to this change involves not just utilizing collaborative tools but redefining how we conceptualize and execute teamwork in a virtual environment.

Seamless Integration of Platforms:

The future lies in the seamless integration of platforms. Professionals are navigating through an ecosystem where tools work in concert rather than isolation. Adaptation involves not just adopting tools like LinkedIn Sales Navigator but integrating them harmoniously into a broader technological landscape.

Evolving customer expectations:

As technology evolves, so do customer expectations. In an era where immediacy and personalization are paramount, businesses must adapt their strategies to meet these expectations. LinkedIn Sales Navigator, as a platform, aligns with this evolution, providing tools to tailor outreach and engagement.

The Call for Digital Literacy: Adapting to technological changes necessitates a level of digital literacy that extends beyond basic proficiency. It requires an understanding of emerging technologies, their implications, and the ability to leverage them strategically. The call is not just for technological adaptation but for a cultural shift towards digital fluency.

The Evolution Of Linkedin Sales Navigator

In the grand tapestry of professional connectivity and

business expansion, few tools have etched a more transformative narrative than LinkedIn Sales Navigator. As we stand on the precipice of delving into its intricacies, it is essential to trace the evolutionary journey that has shaped this platform into the powerhouse of sales and networking it is today.

From Networking Platform to Strategic Tool:

LinkedIn, originally conceived as a professional networking platform, has undergone a metamorphosis. The evolution of LinkedIn Sales Navigator marks a pivotal shift from a passive network-building tool to a dynamic, strategic resource empowering professionals to navigate the complex terrain of sales and business development.

The Rising Demand for Precision:

As professionals sought more precision in their outreach, the need for targeted solutions became apparent. LinkedIn Sales Navigator emerged as a response to this demand, introducing a suite of features meticulously crafted to enable users to identify, connect with, and nurture prospects with unparalleled precision.

Navigating the Digital Landscape:

In a world increasingly defined by digital landscapes, the evolution of LinkedIn Sales Navigator represents a conscious effort to equip professionals with the means to navigate this terrain effectively. Its features align with the paradigm shift towards digital networking, where connections transcend geographical constraints.

The Integration of Intelligent Technologies:

An integral aspect of the evolution lies in the seamless integration of intelligent technologies. From AI-driven recommendations to predictive analytics, LinkedIn Sales Navigator has embraced advancements that empower users with insights, transforming the platform from a static repository of connections to a dynamic tool for informed decision-making.

Empowering Sales Strategies:

The evolution of LinkedIn Sales Navigator signifies a paradigm shift in sales strategies. It transcends traditional methods, offering a comprehensive suite of tools that empower sales professionals to identify opportunities, engage with precision, and foster relationships in a manner that aligns with the nuanced dynamics of modern business.

Catalyzing Global Networking:

With its evolution, LinkedIn Sales Navigator has transcended the confines of regional networking. It has become a catalyst for global connectivity, enabling professionals to build relationships, explore opportunities, and conduct business on an international scale. The platform's global reach mirrors the expansive nature of today's interconnected business landscape.

Adapting to User Feedback:

A hallmark of any evolution is responsiveness to user feedback. The journey of LinkedIn Sales Navigator is characterized by a dedication to comprehending user needs and adapting its features accordingly. It stands as a testament to the platform's dedication to providing a user-centric experience.

Paving the Way for Strategic Networking

In its current iteration, LinkedIn Sales Navigator is not merely a networking tool; it is a strategic ally in the pursuit of professional growth. It empowers users to navigate the intricate web of connections strategically, fostering meaningful relationships that translate into tangible business opportunities.

A Catalyst for Business Growth:

The evolution of LinkedIn Sales Navigator is synonymous with its role as a catalyst for business growth. It has evolved into more than a virtual Rolodex; it is a dynamic engine propelling professionals towards their goals, whether it be lead generation, brand building, or fostering strategic partnerships.

A Glimpse into the Future: As we embark on this journey into the depths of LinkedIn Sales Navigator, it is not just an exploration of its current capabilities but a glimpse into its future potential. The platform's evolution is an ongoing narrative, and the pages ahead will unfold the possibilities that lie on the horizon of professional networking and business development.

With each advancement, LinkedIn Sales Navigator has woven itself into the fabric of modern professional connectivity. As we unravel its intricacies, let us not only understand its current form but also appreciate the evolutionary journey that has shaped it into an indispensable tool for navigating the complex landscapes of sales and business expansion.

CHAPTER ONE

*LinkedIn Sales Navigator:
Navigating the Path to
Business Excellence*

Overview Of The Linkedin Sales Navigator

LinkedIn Sales Navigator is a premier subscription-based tool meticulously crafted to serve as the apex solution for professionals, businesses, and sales teams seeking to navigate the expansive terrain of LinkedIn with precision and purpose. This advanced platform extends beyond the conventional functionalities of LinkedIn, providing a suite of features designed to empower users in their pursuit of strategic networking, lead generation, and business growth.

In essence, LinkedIn Sales Navigator transcends the boundaries of a conventional networking platform. It emerges as an indispensable ally, equipping professionals and businesses with the tools needed to navigate the digital terrain with finesse and acumen. This tool is not merely a feature-rich platform; it is a strategic enabler, transforming LinkedIn from a social network into a dynamic force for business development. As users embark on this journey of exploration, each facet of Sales Navigator unveils new dimensions of strategic prowess, paving the way for unprecedented success in the ever-evolving digital landscape.

Advanced Search and Filters

At the heart of Sales Navigator lies its robust and refined search capabilities. The tool enables users to transcend the limitations of standard searches, offering an array of advanced filters. From industry-specific parameters to granular details such as company size and seniority, Sales Navigator becomes an indispensable compass for pinpointing the most relevant prospects in the vast sea of LinkedIn users.

Lead Recommendations

Sales Navigator leverages sophisticated algorithms to provide users with dynamic lead recommendations. This feature propels networking beyond the confines of immediate connections, presenting users with potential leads aligned with their preferences. This strategic matchmaking accelerates the process of building a high-quality and targeted professional network.

InMail Credits

InMail credits within Sales Navigator serve as a conduit for direct and impactful communication. Users can send personalized messages to prospects even outside their immediate network, fostering meaningful conversations with key decision-makers. This direct line of communication becomes an invaluable asset for cultivating relationships and advancing business objectives.

Real-time Updates

Staying attuned to changes within the professional landscape is imperative for strategic engagement. Sales Navigator provides real-time updates on crucial activities such as job changes and company news, empowering users to engage proactively and position themselves as industry leaders in an ever-evolving market.

Integration with CRM systems

The integration of Sales Navigator with Customer Relationship Management (CRM) systems ensures a seamless flow of insights across the organizational spectrum. This symbiotic relationship enhances the efficiency of sales and marketing teams, providing a holistic view of prospect interactions and contributing to a more cohesive and informed business strategy.

TeamLink

TeamLink, a collaborative feature within Sales Navigator, opens the door to shared connections within a team. This collective network amplifies the prospecting process, facilitating warmer introductions and enhancing the overall efficacy of networking efforts. The power of collaboration becomes a cornerstone for achieving collective business objectives.

Marketing Insights And Advertising Campaigns

Beyond its applications in sales, Sales Navigator extends its utility to the realm of marketing. Users can leverage the platform for targeted advertising campaigns, reaching specific demographics with precision. Additionally, the tool serves as a wellspring of marketing insights, enriching data-driven strategies for comprehensive business growth.

Future Trends and Adaptability

In the ever-evolving landscape of social selling and digital engagement, Sales Navigator stands as a dynamic entity that adapts to emerging trends. From artificial intelligence integrations to responsive user interfaces, the tool remains at the forefront of technological advancements, ensuring users are equipped to navigate future challenges with strategic foresight.

Importance Of The Linkedin Sales Navigator

In the dynamic realm of contemporary commerce, where digital landscapes redefine the contours of success, LinkedIn Sales Navigator emerges as a linchpin for businesses, sales professionals, and marketing teams seeking not just connectivity but precision and strategic advantage. Its transformative effects on important business operations are a testament to its significance.

Precision Targeting Through Advanced Filters:

LinkedIn Sales Navigator transcends conventional LinkedIn functionalities by offering advanced search filters. In the business arena, where precision is paramount, these filters become an invaluable asset. Sales teams can pinpoint prospects with unparalleled accuracy, filtering based on industry, company size, job function, and more. This precision targeting lays the foundation for meaningful connections and strategic business engagements.

Proactive Prospecting and Lead Recommendations:

The tool's sophisticated algorithms dynamically recommend leads aligned with user preferences. In the intricate landscape of sales, where identifying and nurturing leads is a strategic dance, these recommendations streamline the prospecting process. Sales professionals gain access to a curated pool of prospects, accelerating their journey from lead identification to meaningful engagement.

Direct Communication with InMail Credits:

In the realm of sales, timely and direct communication is often the differentiator between success and missed opportunities. LinkedIn Sales Navigator's InMail credits serve as a direct channel to key decision-makers, breaking down communication barriers. This facilitates personalized outreach beyond one's immediate network, fostering genuine connections that form the backbone of successful sales endeavors.

Real-Time Insights for Informed Engagement:

In the fast-paced world of business, staying ahead of industry dynamics is not a luxury but a necessity. LinkedIn Sales Navigator provides real-time updates on key activities, such as job changes and company news. This real-time intelligence empowers sales and marketing teams to engage proactively, demonstrating industry acumen and fortifying their position as thought leaders.

Integration with CRM Systems for Operational Harmony:

The integration of LinkedIn Sales Navigator with Customer Relationship Management (CRM) systems creates a seamless synergy between prospect insights and broader organizational strategy. Sales and marketing teams can operate with enhanced efficiency, ensuring a unified approach to customer interactions. This integration contributes to a more holistic understanding of the customer journey.

Team Collaboration Through TeamLink:

In the collaborative landscape of business, collective networking power often surpasses individual efforts. LinkedIn Sales Navigator's TeamLink feature facilitates collaborative networking by leveraging shared connections within a team. This collaborative approach not only enhances the impact of prospecting but also fosters an environment of shared success and achievement.

Marketing Insights and Targeted Advertising:

Beyond its applications in sales, LinkedIn Sales Navigator extends its utility to the marketing domain. Marketing teams can leverage the platform for targeted advertising campaigns, reaching specific demographics with precision. Moreover, the tool serves as a rich source of marketing insights, enriching data-driven strategies for comprehensive business growth.

CHAPTER TWO

Features Overview of LinkedIn Sales Navigator

LinkedIn Sales Navigator boasts a robust set of features designed to empower professionals, sales teams, and businesses in their pursuit of strategic networking, targeted prospecting, and overall business growth. LinkedIn Sales Navigator, with its diverse features, offers a comprehensive suite of tools and functionalities, making it a versatile and indispensable asset for individuals and teams aiming to navigate the complexities of modern professional networking and business development.

Its key features include the following:

Advanced Search and Filters:

Precision Targeting: Leverage advanced filters to refine searches based on industry, company size, job function, and more.

Granular Criteria: Fine-tune searches to identify prospects with specific attributes crucial for your business objectives.

Lead Recommendations:

- Intelligent Algorithms: Receive dynamic lead suggestions aligned with your preferences and professional goals.

- Efficient Networking: Accelerate the process of building a high-quality network with relevant and strategic connections.

InMail Credits:

Direct Communication: Reach out to decision-makers and key stakeholders outside your immediate network.

Impactful Outreach: Craft personalized messages to foster meaningful connections and advance business objectives.

Real-time Updates:

Timely Insights: Stay informed about changes in target accounts, job transitions, and relevant industry news.

Proactive Engagement: Engage with prospects proactively based on real-time information.

User Interface Walkthrough:

- Optimized Profiles: Enhance your professional presence with an intuitive user interface guiding profile optimization.

- Strategic Positioning: Showcase expertise through compelling headlines and strategically positioned endorsements.

CRM Integration:

Unified Insights: Seamlessly integrate Sales Navigator with CRM systems for a unified view of prospect interactions.

Operational Efficiency: Streamline workflows and enhance

collaboration across sales and marketing functions.

TeamLink:

Collaborative Networking: Access shared connections within your team for more impactful introductions.

Enhanced Outreach: Leverage collective network strength for increased effectiveness in prospecting.

Notes and tags:

Organizational Tools: Add notes and tags to profiles for effective organization and management.

Pipeline Tracking: Streamline interactions, track engagements, and manage sales pipelines with ease.

Saved Leads and Accounts:

Efficient Prospecting: Save leads and accounts for quick access to critical information.

Pipeline Management: Stay organized and monitor key leads efficiently for effective sales pipeline management.

Insights for Marketing Strategies:

Targeted Advertising: Utilize Sales Navigator for targeted advertising campaigns to specific demographics.

Data-Driven Marketing: Extract valuable insights to inform data-driven marketing strategies and comprehensive business growth.

Mobile Accessibility:

On-the-Go Connectivity: Access Sales Navigator features anytime, anywhere with the mobile app.

Real-time Engagement: Stay connected and engaged with prospects while away from your desktop.

Training and support:

Educational Resources: Access training materials and resources for effective utilization.

Customer Support: Receive assistance and guidance through customer support channels.

Sales Navigator Insights:

Performance Metrics: Monitor and analyze your Sales Navigator usage with insights and analytics.

Continuous Improvement: Use data-driven insights to refine your strategies for ongoing improvement.

Advanced Search And Filters

LinkedIn Sales Navigator's Advanced Search and Filters feature stands as a cornerstone, providing users with unparalleled precision in prospect targeting. This robust functionality elevates the prospecting process, allowing professionals, sales teams, and businesses to navigate the expansive LinkedIn ecosystem with finesse and strategic acumen. The Advanced Search and Filters feature in LinkedIn Sales Navigator transcends conventional networking limitations. It empowers users to navigate the expansive LinkedIn ecosystem with surgical precision, ensuring that every prospecting effort is targeted, strategic, and aligned with overarching business objectives. Through its multifaceted capabilities, this feature elevates prospecting from a routine task to a strategic advantage in the pursuit of meaningful professional connections and sustained business growth.

Precision Targeting:

Granular Criteria: Users can refine searches based on a myriad of criteria, including industry, company size, location, job function, and more.

Customized Searches: Tailor searches to align with specific business goals, ensuring that each query is finely tuned to the desired prospect profile.

Industry and Company-Specific Filters:

Industry Focus: Narrow down searches to specific industries, facilitating targeted outreach to prospects within a particular business sector.

Company Size Criteria: Filter results based on company size, enabling users to focus on enterprises that align with their strategic objectives.

Job Function and Seniority Levels:

Job Role Precision: Target prospects based on their specific job functions, ensuring relevance in outreach efforts.

Seniority Selection: Filter results by seniority levels, allowing users to connect with decision-makers or influencers based on their organizational hierarchy.

Geographic Filters:

Localized Prospecting: Define searches based on geographic parameters, facilitating outreach to prospects in specific regions or locations.

Global Reach: Seamlessly switch between local and global searches to accommodate diverse business needs.

Boolean Search Techniques:

Logical Operators: Harness Boolean search capabilities for more complex queries, combining keywords and phrases to refine search results.

Customized Queries: Employ AND, OR, and NOT operators to create tailored searches, offering a higher degree of specificity.

Saved searches for efficiency:

Time-Saving Functionality: Save frequently used search queries for quick and efficient prospecting in subsequent sessions.

Automated Updates: Receive notifications and updates when new prospects match saved search criteria, ensuring ongoing relevance.

Company and job change alerts:

Real-time Updates: Stay informed about changes within target accounts, including job changes and company updates.

Proactive Engagement: Act on real-time information to engage with prospects during crucial moments of transition or growth.

Team Collaboration:

Shared Filters: Collaborate with team members by sharing search filters, fostering a collective approach to prospecting.

Enhanced Outreach: Leverage shared insights to enhance team-wide outreach efforts and maximize impact.

Smart Suggestions for Enhanced Results:

Intelligent Recommendations: Benefit from smart suggestions that enhance search parameters based on user behavior and preferences.

Efficient Prospecting: Receive dynamic recommendations to discover new prospects aligned with strategic goals.

Lead Recommendations

In the dynamic realm of professional networking, LinkedIn Sales Navigator's Lead Recommendations emerge as a sophisticated tool, redefining the landscape of strategic connections. This feature goes above and beyond conventional networking strategies by providing users with personalized and dynamic insights for creating a strong and strategically aligned network. In essence, LinkedIn Sales Navigator's Lead Recommendations feature transforms networking into a strategic venture guided by intelligence and adaptability. As users leverage this feature, they embark on a journey of building a network that not only meets immediate needs but also evolves in sync with their professional growth. Elevate your networking strategy with lead recommendations, where each connection made becomes a purposeful step toward broader horizons and sustained success.

Dynamic Suggestions for Relevant Connections:

Intelligent Algorithms: The Lead Recommendations feature employs advanced algorithms to dynamically suggest potential connections based on user preferences and historical interactions.

Continuous Refinement: The algorithm evolves over time, adapting to changing user needs and refining recommendations for continuous relevance.

Accelerating network building:

Efficiency in Networking: Lead Recommendations expedites the process of building a high-quality network by presenting users with prospects highly aligned with their industry and professional goals.

Strategic Connections: Users can swiftly identify and connect with individuals strategically relevant to their business pursuits, creating a network of value.

Contextually relevant networking:

• Industry Alignment: Tailored to specific industries, lead recommendations ensure that suggested connections align contextually with users' professional objectives.

• Job Function Focus: Recommendations also consider job functions, providing a nuanced understanding of potential leads for more meaningful connections.

Proactive Networking Opportunities:

Anticipatory Connections: Receive suggestions for potential leads even before initiating searches, enabling proactive networking opportunities.

Real-time Adaptation: Lead recommendations adapt in real-time, reflecting changes in user behavior and ensuring suggestions remain timely and relevant.

Diverse Perspectives and Exploration:

Expanding Networks: Users can explore connections beyond immediate circles, gaining diverse perspectives and broadening the scope of their professional network.

Insights into New Industries: Gain insights into industries beyond the user's immediate focus, fostering exploration and potential collaboration in new sectors.

Customization for Targeted Outreach:

Tailoring Suggestions: Lead recommendations can be customized based on specific criteria, aligning suggestions with targeted prospecting efforts.

Efficient Outreach: Ensure that outreach efforts are not only strategic but also efficient, maximizing the impact of connection requests and engagement.

Adaptive Learning Mechanism:

User Behavior Analysis: The Lead Recommendations feature learns continuously from user behavior, adapting and refining suggestions based on patterns and interactions.

Personalized Experience: Users benefit from a personalized networking experience with suggestions closely aligned with their professional interests.

Streamlined Decision-Making:

Informed Connection Choices: Lead Recommendations provide users with the information needed to make informed decisions about which connections to pursue.

Effortless Networking: The streamlined decision-making process ensures that networking efforts are purposeful and seamlessly integrated into the user's professional journey.

InMail Credits

LinkedIn Sales Navigator's InMail Credits feature is a powerful tool that facilitates direct and impactful communication with key decision-makers, influencers, and prospects beyond your immediate network. InMail Credits go beyond traditional messaging, providing users with a means to craft personalized messages that can be instrumental in fostering meaningful connections and advancing business objectives.

LinkedIn Sales Navigator's InMail Credits feature is not just a messaging tool; it's a strategic resource that empowers professionals to initiate high-impact conversations and cultivate relationships beyond the boundaries of their immediate network. Whether reaching out to potential clients, partners, or industry influencers, InMail Credits serve as a key component of a comprehensive outreach strategy within the dynamic landscape of professional networking.

Direct Communication Beyond Network Limits:

Access to Decision-Makers: InMail Credits allow users to reach out directly to individuals who may not be within their immediate network.

Key Stakeholder Engagement: Engage with decision-makers, influencers, and relevant prospects, opening avenues for impactful conversations.

Crafting personalized messages:

Tailored Communication: InMail Credits empower users to craft personalized and compelling messages that go beyond the constraints of standard connection requests.

Impactful First Impressions: Make a lasting first impression with messages that resonate with the recipient's professional context and objectives.

Strategic Outreach Opportunities:

Initiating Conversations: Use InMail Credits strategically to initiate conversations with prospects who align closely with your business goals.

Access to Exclusive Networks: InMail Credits provide a gateway to engaging with individuals in exclusive networks, ensuring your outreach is targeted and purposeful.

Overcoming Communication Barriers:

Bypassing Connection Restrictions: InMail Credits allow users to send messages to individuals outside their immediate network without the need for a prior connection.

Enhancing Reach: Overcome communication barriers and extend your reach to a broader audience, amplifying the impact of your outreach efforts.

Personalization for Effective Engagement:

Tailoring Messages: Craft messages that are tailored to the recipient's profile, interests, and professional background.

Increased Response Rates: Personalized communication increases the likelihood of positive responses, creating a foundation for meaningful interactions.

InMail Analytics for Performance Tracking:

Performance Insights: Gain insights into the performance of your InMail messages through the analytics provided by Sales Navigator.

Iterative Refinement: Use analytics to refine your messaging strategy, ensuring continuous improvement in the effectiveness of your outreach.

Strategic Relationship Building:

Building Rapport: InMail Credits are a strategic tool for initiating and building rapport with potential clients, partners, or collaborators.

Cultivating Meaningful Connections: Establish a foundation for meaningful connections that can lead to long-term relationships and business opportunities.

Usage Flexibility with InMail Credits:

No Connection Requirements: InMail Credits provide the flexibility to communicate with anyone on LinkedIn, irrespective of existing connections.

Controlled Outreach: Users have control over when and how to use their InMail Credits, allowing for strategic and measured outreach.

InMail Response Guarantee:

Credit Refund for Non-Responses: Sales Navigator offers a guarantee that if your InMail doesn't receive a response within 7 days, the credit used will be refunded for future use.

Risk Mitigation: Provides assurance and risk mitigation for users, encouraging proactive and confident outreach.

Real-time Updates

LinkedIn Sales Navigator's real-time updates feature serves as a dynamic tool that keeps users abreast of changes and activities within their target accounts and the broader professional landscape. In a fast-paced business environment, this feature empowers professionals to engage proactively, make informed decisions, and position themselves as industry thought leaders.

LinkedIn Sales Navigator's Real-Time Updates feature transcends conventional monitoring by providing users with a real-time pulse on their professional landscape. In a world where timing is crucial, this feature becomes an invaluable asset, enabling professionals to navigate changes, capitalize on opportunities, and engage with their network in a manner that is both strategic and impactful.

Timely Insights into Target Accounts:

Job Changes: Receive instant notifications when key decision-makers within your target accounts undergo job changes.

Company Updates: Stay informed about significant developments within target companies, ensuring your outreach is timely and relevant.

Proactive Engagement Opportunities:

Strategic Networking: Real-time updates provide opportunities for proactive engagement with professionals during crucial moments of transition or change.

Thought Leadership Positioning: Engage with timely and relevant content, positioning yourself as a thought leader within your industry.

Industry News and Trends:

Timely Industry Insights: Stay updated on industry trends, news, and events, allowing you to align your strategies with the broader professional landscape.

Strategic Decision-Making: Use real-time industry information to make informed decisions and anticipate changes that may impact your business.

Notifications on Relevant Activities:

Customized Alerts: Receive notifications tailored to your specific criteria, ensuring that you stay focused on activities most relevant to your business objectives.

Flexible Customization: Customize alerts based on factors

such as job changes, company news, and other activities critical to your prospecting efforts.

Timely Outreach Opportunities:

Congratulatory Outreach: Capitalize on job changes by sending congratulatory messages to individuals in new roles, fostering positive connections.

Relevant Conversations: Engage in conversations that are timely and pertinent, increasing the likelihood of meaningful interactions.

Comprehensive prospect tracking:

Holistic View of Prospects: Real-time updates provide a holistic view of your prospects, helping you understand their professional journeys and interests.

Enhanced Relationship Management: Use insights to build stronger relationships and tailor your interactions based on real-time activities.

Automated Monitoring for Efficiency:

Effortless Monitoring: Real-time updates automate the process of monitoring key accounts and industry developments, saving time and effort.

Streamlined Workflow: Enjoy a streamlined workflow with automated notifications, allowing you to focus on strategic engagement rather than manual tracking.

Competitive Intelligence:

Insights into Competitors: Monitor the activities of competitors and industry players, gaining valuable intelligence for strategic positioning.

Adaptive Strategies: Adapt your strategies based on real-time information, ensuring a proactive and competitive approach in the market.

Thought Leadership and Content Sharing:

Timely Content Sharing: Share industry-relevant content at the right moment, leveraging real-time updates to maximize visibility.

Building Authority: Position yourself as an authority by engaging in conversations and sharing insights when your audience is most receptive.

User Interface Walkthrough

LinkedIn Sales Navigator's user interface is designed to be intuitive and empowering, providing users with a seamless experience as they navigate the platform. This walkthrough offers a comprehensive guide to the key elements of the user interface, ensuring that professionals can maximize their use of Sales Navigator for strategic networking and business growth.

LinkedIn Sales Navigator's user interface is an embodiment of accessibility and strategic functionality. As you navigate through its features, you'll find that each element is meticulously designed to enhance your networking experience, streamline your workflow, and empower you with the insights needed for impactful decision-making. Whether you're exploring lead recommendations, engaging in direct communication, or leveraging collaborative features, the Sales Navigator interface is your gateway to unlocking the full potential of strategic networking and business development.

Dashboard Overview:

Personalized Homepage: The dashboard provides a snapshot of personalized insights, including updates on saved leads, accounts, and recommended leads.

Navigation Bar: Access key features such as Home, Network, Leads, and more from the top navigation bar.

Advanced Search and Filters:

Refined Prospect Targeting: Utilize the advanced search and filters to precisely target prospects based on criteria like industry, company size, and job function.

Boolean Search: Employ Boolean operators for more complex and customized queries.

Lead Recommendations:

Dynamic Suggestions: Explore the Lead Recommendations section for dynamic suggestions based on your preferences and professional goals.

Efficient Networking: Accelerate the process of building a high-quality network with leads strategically aligned with your objectives.

InMail Credits:

Direct Communication: Access InMail Credits for direct communication with decision-makers and key stakeholders outside your immediate network.

Message Tracking: Track the performance of your InMail messages and refine your outreach strategy.

Real-time Updates:

Timely Notifications: Stay informed about changes in

target accounts, job transitions, and industry news with real-time updates.

Customized Alerts: Customize notifications based on your specific criteria for a personalized experience.

CRM Integration:

Unified Insights: Seamlessly integrate Sales Navigator with CRM systems for a unified view of prospect interactions.

Operational Efficiency: Streamline workflows and enhance collaboration across sales and marketing functions.

TeamLink Collaboration:

Shared Connections: Leverage TeamLink for collaborative networking, accessing shared connections within your team.

Enhanced Outreach: Amplify the impact of prospecting through collaborative efforts.

Notes and tags:

Organized Interaction: Add notes and tags to profiles for effective organization and management of connections.

Pipeline Tracking: Streamline interactions, track engagements, and manage sales pipelines efficiently.

Saved Leads and Accounts:

Efficient Prospecting: Save leads and accounts for quick access to critical information.

Pipeline Management: Stay organized and monitor key leads for effective sales pipeline management.

Mobile Accessibility:

On-the-Go Connectivity: Access Sales Navigator features anytime, anywhere with the mobile app.

Real-time Engagement: Stay connected and engaged with prospects while away from your desktop.

Training and support:

Educational Resources: Explore training materials and resources for effective utilization.

Customer Support: Access assistance and guidance through customer support channels.

Sales Navigator Insights:

Performance Metrics: Monitor and analyze your Sales Navigator usage with insights and analytics.

Continuous Improvement: Use data-driven insights to refine your strategies for ongoing improvement.

CHAPTER THREE

Setting Up Your LinkedIn
Sales Navigator Account

Setting up your LinkedIn Sales Navigator account involves several steps to ensure that you can maximize the platform's features for effective sales and networking. Note that the specific steps and features may vary based on updates made to the LinkedIn Sales Navigator platform. Always refer to the official LinkedIn Sales Navigator website and resources for the most accurate and up-to-date information.

Here's a step-by-step guide to help you set up your LinkedIn Sales Navigator account:

Step 1: Access LinkedIn Sales Navigator

Visit the official LinkedIn Sales Navigator website: https://business.linkedin.com/sales-solutions/sales-navigator.

Step 2: Choose a Plan

Explore the available subscription plans (professional, team, or enterprise) based on your needs.

Click on the "Start your free trial" or "Try for free" button associated with your chosen plan.

Step 3: Sign In to Your LinkedIn Account

If you already have a LinkedIn account, sign in with your credentials.

If you don't have a LinkedIn account, you'll need to create one by providing the necessary information.

Step 4: Complete the Onboarding Process

Follow the on-screen instructions to complete the onboarding process.

LinkedIn may prompt you to provide additional information about your role, industry, and preferences to tailor your Sales Navigator experience.

Step 5: Set Up Your Profile

Ensure that your LinkedIn profile is complete and optimized for professional networking.

Add a professional photo, update your headline, and provide a compelling summary.

Step 6: Connect Your CRM (Optional)

If you use a customer relationship management (CRM) system, consider connecting it to Sales Navigator for streamlined insights.

Follow the prompts to integrate your CRM, if applicable.

Step 7: Explore Sales Navigator Features

Familiarize yourself with the Sales Navigator interface, including the navigation bar, search filters, lead recommendations, and more.

Take advantage of the platform's features, such as InMail credits, real-time updates, and advanced search capabilities.

Step 8: Customize Preferences

Adjust your Sales Navigator settings to match your preferences.

Customize email notifications, privacy settings, and communication preferences.

Step 9: Utilize Training Resources

Explore the training resources provided by LinkedIn Sales Solutions.

Take advantage of webinars, tutorials, and guides to enhance your understanding of the platform.

Step 10: Start Prospecting and Networking

Begin using Sales Navigator to search for leads, engage with prospects, and build meaningful connections.

Leverage InMail credits for direct communication and explore advanced search filters for targeted prospecting.

Step 11: Monitor and iterate

Regularly monitor the performance of your activities on Sales Navigator.

Use insights and analytics to refine your strategies for ongoing improvement.

Optimizing Your Profile for Sales

Optimizing your LinkedIn profile for sales on Sales Navigator is crucial for making a strong and impactful impression on potential prospects. A well-optimized profile increases your visibility, builds credibility, and encourages meaningful connections.

By implementing these strategies, you can create a compelling LinkedIn profile that positions you as a knowledgeable and trustworthy professional in the eyes of your prospects on LinkedIn Sales Navigator. Remember to adapt and refine your profile based on changes in your role, accomplishments, or industry trends.

Follow the following step-by-step guide to optimize your LinkedIn profile for sales:

Professional Profile Photo:

Use a high-quality and professional profile photo.

Ensure that your face is well-lit and that you appear approachable and friendly.

Compelling Headline:

Craft a headline that clearly communicates your role and expertise.

Include keywords relevant to your industry and sales focus.

Informative Summary:

Write a compelling summary that highlights your experience, skills, and what you bring to the table.

Clearly articulate your value proposition and how you can help potential clients.

Customized LinkedIn URL:

Create a custom LinkedIn URL that is easy to remember and includes your name.

This makes it easier for people to find and connect with you.

Detailed Experience Section:

Provide detailed information about your current and past roles.

Highlight specific achievements, key responsibilities, and measurable results.

Skills and endorsements:

List relevant skills related to your sales expertise.

Encourage colleagues and connections to endorse your skills to build credibility.

Recommendations:

Seek recommendations from colleagues, clients, or managers to showcase your professional strengths.

Recommendations add authenticity and credibility to your profile.

Industry-Optimized Keywords:

Integrate industry-specific keywords throughout your profile to improve searchability.

Use terms that potential clients might use when searching for your services.

Media and Documents:

Add media and documents to showcase your work, presentations, or case studies.

Visual elements enhance the appeal of your profile.

Sales Navigator Settings:

Set your Sales Navigator preferences to align with your sales goals.

Adjust privacy settings and communication preferences.

Regular Updates:

Keep your profile updated with your latest achievements, projects, and responsibilities.

Regular updates show that your profile is active and engaged.

Engagement with Content:

Share and engage with relevant content in your industry.

Participate in discussions and showcase your knowledge.

InMail and Connection Requests:

Craft personalized and compelling email messages when reaching out to prospects.

Send connection requests with a personalized note explaining the value of connecting.

Utilize Sales Navigator Features:

Leverage Sales Navigator features such as saved leads, lead recommendations, and real-time updates.

Make the most of advanced search filters for targeted prospecting.

Professional Headline:

Your headline is one of the first things people see. Make it clear, concise, and focused on the value you provide.

Showcasing relevant achievements:

Highlight specific achievements, awards, or recognitions that demonstrate your expertise in sales.

Education and Certifications:

Include relevant education and certifications that showcase your qualifications.

Consistent Branding:

Maintain consistency in branding across your LinkedIn profile and other professional platforms.

Engage with recommendations:

Thank people for endorsements and recommendations, and reciprocate when appropriate.

Clear Call-to-Action:

Include a clear call-to-action in your summary or contact section, inviting potential clients to connect or learn more about your services.

Connecting Sales Navigator With Crm Systems

Connecting LinkedIn Sales Navigator with Customer Relationship Management (CRM) systems enhances your sales strategy by providing a unified platform for managing relationships, insights, and communications.

By seamlessly connecting LinkedIn Sales Navigator with your CRM system, you create a more efficient and streamlined sales process, enabling you to leverage the power of both platforms for successful relationship management and business development.

By seamlessly connecting LinkedIn Sales Navigator with your CRM system, you create a more efficient and streamlined sales process, enabling you to leverage the power of both platforms for successful relationship management and business development. While the specific steps may vary based on your CRM and Sales Navigator versions, there are general rules to follow on how to connect Sales Navigator with a CRM system. They include the following:

Choose a supported CRM:

Ensure that your CRM system is compatible with LinkedIn Sales Navigator. Commonly supported CRMs include Salesforce, Microsoft Dynamics 365, HubSpot, and more.

Login to LinkedIn Sales Navigator:

Access your LinkedIn Sales Navigator account using your credentials.

Navigate to CRM Integration Settings:

Look for the "Settings" or "Preferences" section in LinkedIn Sales Navigator.

Select CRM Integration:

Find the option related to CRM integration. This may be labeled as "Integrations," "CRM Settings," or something similar.

Choose your CRM:

Select your CRM system from the list of supported integrations.

Authorize Connection:

LinkedIn Sales Navigator will prompt you to authorize the connection to your CRM. Follow the on-screen instructions to grant access.

Provide CRM credentials:

Enter the necessary credentials (username and password) for your CRM account.

Map Fields:

LinkedIn Sales Navigator will ask you to map fields between Sales Navigator and your CRM. This ensures that data is synchronized correctly.

Map standard fields such as name, email, company, etc.

Configure Sync Settings:

Configure synchronization settings, such as how often data should be synchronized between Sales Navigator and your CRM.

Review and confirm:

Review the settings and confirm the integration. This may involve a final authorization step.

Sync Existing Contacts:

Some integrations allow you to sync existing contacts from your CRM to Sales Navigator. This step can help you leverage LinkedIn insights for your current contacts.

Test the integration:

Test the integration by updating a contact in your CRM and checking if the changes reflect in Sales Navigator (and vice versa).

Explore Integrated Features:

Once the integration is successful, explore the features offered by the CRM-Sales Navigator integration.

This may include accessing LinkedIn profiles from your CRM, viewing Sales Navigator insights within the CRM, and more.

Utilize insights for sales activities:

Leverage the integrated insights to inform your sales activities, personalize outreach, and enhance engagement with leads and contacts.

Regularly monitor and update:

Regularly monitor the integration to ensure that the data remains synchronized.

Update any settings or mappings as needed based on changes in your CRM or Sales Navigator.

Seek support from the CRM provider:

Consult the support documentation that your CRM system has provided if you run into problems.

Reach out to your CRM provider for assistance with specific integration challenges.

Note:

Refer to the specific documentation that LinkedIn Sales Navigator and your CRM have provided for detailed instructions as integration steps may vary depending on the CRM platform.

Ensure that your LinkedIn Sales Navigator account has the necessary permissions for CRM integration.

CHAPTER FOUR

*Leveraging Advanced
Search for Prospecting*

Target Audience Identification

Leveraging LinkedIn Sales Navigator's Advanced Search is a powerful strategy for identifying and prospecting your target audience. This feature allows you to refine your search criteria to pinpoint individuals who meet specific qualifications, making your outreach more targeted and effective. LinkedIn Sales Navigator's Advanced Search is a dynamic tool that allows for precise targeting, helping you identify and connect with your ideal audience. By strategically using the filters and features available, you can streamline your prospecting efforts and increase the likelihood of engaging with individuals who are genuinely interested in your products or services.

**To use Advanced Search for prospecting, follow
these guidelines.**

Access Advanced Search:

Log in to your LinkedIn Sales Navigator account.

Navigate to the "Search" bar at the top and click on "All Filters."

Define your search criteria:

Specify the criteria that align with your target audience. Consider factors such as:

Keywords: Include relevant keywords related to job titles, skills, or industries.

Location: Refine your search based on geographic locations.

Company: Specify the target companies or industries you're interested in.

Job Title: Identify specific job titles that match your ideal prospects.

Industry and Company Size Filters:

Utilize the "industry" and "company size" filters to narrow down your search to specific sectors and company scales.

This is particularly useful for B2B sales targeting specific industries or company types.

Job Function and Seniority Level:

Refine your search based on job functions and seniority levels.

Tailor your outreach depending on whether you're targeting decision-makers, influencers, or specific roles within organizations.

Save Your Search:

Once you've configured your search with the desired criteria, consider saving it for future use.

Saved searches enable you to quickly access and rerun searches without re-entering criteria.

Boolean Search Techniques:

Harness the power of boolean operators (AND, OR, NOT) for more complex queries.

Combine keywords strategically to fine-tune your search results.

Use "Connections" and "Lead Filters":

Set filters based on your existing connections to identify second- and third-degree connections.

Leverage "Lead Filters" to focus on specific traits, such as decision-makers or influencers.

Apply "Account" filters:

If you're interested in targeting specific companies, use the "Account" filters to refine your search based on company names.

Regularly refine your criteria:

Prospective requirements may evolve, so regularly revisit and refine your search criteria.

Stay adaptable to changes in your industry or target market.

Review Search Results:

Review the search results to ensure they align with your target audience.

Explore profiles to gather insights that can inform your outreach strategy.

Initiate Connections and InMail Messages:

Connect with individuals who match your target audience

criteria.

Craft personalized email messages that clearly communicate the value you offer.

Engage with content:

Follow and interact with the relevant content that your prospects share.

This can help establish rapport and demonstrate your interest in their industry.

Track and analyze results:

Monitor the performance of your outreach efforts.

Analyze which criteria are yielding the best results and adjust your strategy accordingly.

Explore team collaboration:

If you're part of a sales team, consider using the team collaboration features to share and collaborate on prospecting efforts.

Using filters effectively

Leveraging LinkedIn Sales Navigator's Advanced Search with effective use of filters is key to honing in on your target audience and optimizing your prospecting efforts. By strategically applying various filters, you can refine your search results to identify individuals who align closely with your ideal prospects. By using LinkedIn Sales

Navigator's Advanced Search filters effectively, you can significantly enhance the precision of your prospecting efforts. These filters empower you to target individuals with a high potential for conversion, ultimately leading to more meaningful connections and successful business relationships. Regularly assess and adjust your filtering criteria based on the evolving needs of your sales strategy.

Follow these guidelines to use filters effectively for prospecting:

Location Filters:

Country, Region, and Postal Code: Specify the geographic location where your target audience is concentrated.

Radius Search: Use the radius search option to target a specific distance around a location.

Keywords and Boolean Operators:

Keywords: Incorporate relevant keywords related to job titles, skills, or industries.

Boolean operators (AND, OR, NOT): Combine keywords strategically for more nuanced searches.

Company Filters:

Company Name: If you have specific companies in mind, use the "Company" filter to narrow your search.

Company Size: Refine your search based on the size of the companies you're targeting.

Job Title and Function:

Job Title: Specify the job titles of individuals you want to target.

Job Function: Refine your search based on broader job

functions within organizations.

Seniority Level:

Seniority Level: Filter your search based on seniority levels, targeting decision-makers or influencers.

Industry Filters:

Industry: Narrow down your search to specific industries relevant to your target audience.

Schools and degrees:

Schools: If education is a relevant criterion, filter by specific schools.

Degrees: Specify the degrees or qualifications that align with your target audience.

Years of Experience:

Experience Level: Refine your search based on the number of years of professional experience.

Company Relationship Filters:

Connection Level: Filter by your existing connections or degree of connection separation.

TeamLink Connections: Leverage shared connections within your sales team.

Lead Filters:

Function within Company: Target individuals based on their role within a company.

Role on Account: Specify roles relevant to your sales goals.

Groups and Associations:

Group Membership: Filter by membership in specific LinkedIn groups.

Association Memberships: If applicable, filter based on memberships in professional associations.

Date of Job Change:

Date Posted: If timely information is crucial, use the "Date Posted" filter to focus on recent updates.

Saved Search Criteria:

Save Searches: Save your search criteria for future use, allowing for quick access to refined prospecting.

Review Search Results:

Quality vs. Quantity: Assess the quality of search results rather than focusing solely on quantity.

Refine Criteria as Needed: If results are too broad or too narrow, adjust your filters accordingly.

Utilize real-time insights:

Leverage real-time updates and insights to stay informed about changes in your target audience's profiles.

Combine multiple filters:

Combine multiple filters to create a comprehensive search that reflects your ideal prospect profile.

Iterate and experiment:

Regularly iterate and experiment with different filter combinations to optimize your prospecting strategy.

InMail and Connection Outreach:

Use the insights gathered from your filtered searches to craft personalized InMail messages or connection requests.

Boolean Search Techniques

Leveraging Boolean search techniques in LinkedIn Sales Navigator's Advanced Search can significantly enhance your prospecting capabilities by allowing you to create more nuanced and specific queries. Boolean operators (AND, OR, NOT) enable you to combine keywords and criteria for a more refined search.

By mastering Boolean search techniques, you can create highly specific and targeted searches, enabling you to identify prospects that closely match your ideal audience. Regularly experiment with different combinations of operators and keywords to refine your search queries based on the evolving needs of your sales strategy.

Use Boolean search techniques effectively for prospecting with these top-notch guidelines.

AND Operator (+):

Use Case: Combine multiple keywords to narrow down your search.

Example: Sales + Manager

Result: This will show profiles containing both the terms "sales" and "manager."

OR Operator (|):

Use Case: Expand your search by including profiles with any of the specified terms.

Example: Sales and Marketing

Result: This will show profiles with either "Sales" or "Marketing" or both.

NOT Operator (-):

Use Case: Exclude specific terms from your search to make it more targeted.

Example: Sales Assistant

Result: This will show profiles with "Sales" but exclude those with "Assistant."

Parentheses for grouping:

Use Case: Group terms to create more complex search queries.

Example: (Sales | Marketing) AND Manager

Result: This will show profiles with either "Sales" or "Marketing" and "Manager."

Quotation Marks for Exact Phrases:

Use Case: Search for an exact phrase rather than individual keywords.

Example: "Digital Marketing Manager"

Result: This will show profiles with the exact phrase "Digital Marketing Manager."

Wildcard (*) for Variations:

Use Case: Include variations of a keyword in your search.

Example: Engin*

Result: This will show profiles with variations like "engineer," "engineering," etc.

Combining Operators:

Use Case: Create highly specific queries by combining multiple operators.

Example: ("Product Manager" | "Product Owner") AND

(Software | Technology)

Result: This will show profiles with either "Product Manager" or "Product Owner" in the software or technology industry.

Boolean Search in Job Titles:

Use Case: Refine searches specifically within job titles.

Example: ("Business Development" | "Sales") AND (Manager | Director)

Result: This will show profiles with job titles containing "Business Development" or "Sales" and "Manager" or "Director."

Boolean Search for Skills:

Use Case: Target profiles based on specific skills.

Example: (Java, Python) AND "Machine Learning"

Result: This will show profiles with skills in either Java or Python and expertise in "machine learning."

Location-based Boolean Search:

Use Case: Combine locations for broader or more localized searches.

Example: (New York, San Francisco) AND (Sales, Marketing)

Result: This will show profiles in New York or San Francisco with backgrounds in sales or marketing.

Refining Boolean Searches Over Time:

Use Case: Refine your Boolean searches based on evolving prospecting needs.

Example: (Cloud Computing | "Data Science") AND (Manager | Director)—Assistant

Result: This will show profiles related to cloud computing or data science in managerial or directorial roles, excluding those with "Assistant."

Experiment and iterate:

Use Case: Regularly experiment with different combinations and iterate based on the effectiveness of your searches.

Example: (Digital Marketing | SEO | SEM) AND "Content Strategy"—Intern

CHAPTER FIVE

Lead Recommendations and
Building Connections

Understanding Lead Recommendations

LinkedIn Sales Navigator's Lead Recommendations is a valuable feature designed to streamline your prospecting efforts by suggesting potential leads based on your preferences and business objectives. This feature employs advanced algorithms and machine learning to analyze your existing connections, saved leads, and account preferences. Understanding how to leverage lead recommendations effectively can significantly enhance your ability to build meaningful connections. Lead recommendations offer a dynamic and efficient way to expand your network with relevant and high-potential connections. By understanding how this feature works and integrating it into your prospecting routine, you can build a robust network that aligns closely with your business objectives and establishes a foundation for successful professional relationships.

Accessing Lead Recommendations:

Navigate to the "Home" tab on your LinkedIn Sales

Navigator dashboard.

Look for the "Recommended Leads" or "Lead Recommendations" section.

How Lead Recommendations Work:

LinkedIn's algorithms analyze your current connections, saved leads, and account criteria.

Suggestions are based on factors such as job titles, industries, and mutual connections.

Customizing Recommendations:

Refine your lead recommendations by adjusting your saved leads and account preferences.

Click on "See More Leads" to access additional suggestions.

Filters for targeted recommendations:

Utilize advanced search filters to customize lead recommendations further.

Apply filters such as industry, company size, and location for more targeted results.

Understanding Recommendation Criteria:

LinkedIn considers factors like shared connections, industry relevance, and job titles in its recommendations.

Recommendations are designed to align with your sales and networking objectives.

Reviewing lead profiles:

Click on individual profiles within the Lead Recommendations to review detailed information.

Assess whether the suggested leads align with your target

audience and business goals.

Engaging with recommendations:

Send personalized connection requests to recommended leads.

Craft a compelling message explaining the value of connecting.

Building a Diverse Network:

Use lead recommendations to diversify your network by connecting with professionals in different industries and roles.

This can open up new opportunities and perspectives.

Leveraging TeamLink Connections:

If you're part of a sales team, explore lead recommendations with TeamLink connections.

Collaborate with your team to build connections and enhance outreach efforts.

Combining Lead Recommendations with InMail:

If a lead is particularly relevant, consider using InMail to send a direct and personalized message.

Introduce yourself and express your interest in connecting.

Monitoring and iterating:

Regularly review and monitor the performance of your lead recommendations.

Iterate and adjust your saved leads and preferences based on the evolving needs of your prospecting strategy.

Building Relationships, Not Just Connections:

Focus on building meaningful relationships rather than simply amassing connections.

Engage with your network by sharing valuable content and participating in relevant discussions.

LinkedIn Sales Navigator Mobile App:

Access lead recommendations on the go through the LinkedIn Sales Navigator mobile app.

Stay connected and responsive, even when away from your desktop.

Understanding Mutual Connections:

When reviewing lead recommendations, pay attention to the mutual connections you share with potential leads.

Leverage mutual connections for warm introductions and enhanced relationship-building.

Incorporating Recommendations into Sales Strategy:

Integrate lead recommendations seamlessly into your overall sales strategy.

Use the insights gained to inform your outreach and engagement efforts.

Strategies For Building Connections

Building connections on LinkedIn is a strategic process that involves more than just sending connection requests. By implementing thoughtful and personalized strategies, you can foster meaningful connections that contribute to your professional growth and business objectives.

Here are effective strategies for building connections on LinkedIn:

Optimize your profile:

Ensure your LinkedIn profile is complete, professional, and showcases your expertise.

Use a high-quality profile picture, craft a compelling headline, and write a detailed summary.

Define Your Target Audience:

Clearly identify your target audience and industry.

Use LinkedIn Sales Navigator's Lead Recommendations and Advanced Search to find relevant profiles.

Personalize connection requests:

Craft personalized connection requests for each individual.

Mention common interests, mutual connections, or shared experiences.

Engage with content:

Share relevant content, articles, and updates on your LinkedIn feed.

Engage with content from your network by liking, commenting, and sharing.

Participate in groups:

Join and actively participate in LinkedIn groups related to your industry.

Contribute to discussions and showcase your expertise.

Utilize Lead Recommendations:

Leverage LinkedIn Sales Navigator's Lead Recommendations to discover potential connections.

Review and connect with individuals aligned with your business goals.

Warm Introductions:

If possible, seek warm introductions from mutual connections.

Request introductions that highlight the shared interests or benefits of connecting.

Send personalized messages:

After connecting, send personalized welcome messages.

Express your interest in the connection and open the door for further communication.

Express Gratitude:

Thank new connections for connecting with you.

Show appreciation for their time and express your eagerness to learn from each other.

Highlight shared Interests:

Identify and highlight shared interests or commonalities in your outreach.

This helps create a sense of connection and shared purpose.

Be Genuine and Authentic:

Be genuine in your interactions and communications.

Avoid generic or automated messages; instead, be authentic and personable.

Connect through Comments:

Engage with individuals by leaving thoughtful comments on their posts.

This can spark conversations and make your connection request more recognizable.

Utilize LinkedIn Events:

Attend and engage with LinkedIn Events related to your industry.

Connect with participants and speakers after the event.

Offer Value:

Demonstrate the value you bring to your connections.

Share insights, resources, or offer assistance based on your expertise.

Regularly Review Connections:

Periodically review your connections and identify areas for further engagement.

Keep your network dynamic and aligned with your evolving goals.

Create and share compelling content:

Showcase your expertise by creating and sharing valuable content.

Position yourself as a thought leader in your industry.

Acknowledge Milestones:

Congratulate connections on work anniversaries, promotions, or other milestones.

This demonstrates your genuine interest in their professional journey.

Provide Recommendations:

Write thoughtful recommendations for connections when appropriate.

This adds credibility to your profile and strengthens your professional relationships.

Stay Professional in Communication:

Maintain a professional tone in all communications.

Be respectful, responsive, and considerate in your interactions.

Follow Up and Nurture Connections:

Regularly follow up with your connections through messages or comments.

Nurture relationships over time to build trust and rapport.

Utilizing Teamlink For Warm Introductions

LinkedIn Sales Navigator's TeamLink is a powerful feature that allows you to leverage the collective network of your sales team for warm introductions and enhanced networking. By utilizing TeamLink effectively, you can tap into your team's connections to expand your network and build valuable relationships.

By effectively utilizing TeamLink for warm introductions, you can tap into the collective power of your sales team's network, expanding your reach and creating valuable connections within your target audience. Collaborate with your team, personalize your outreach, and leverage shared connections to build a network that contributes to your professional success and business objectives.

To enjoy TeamLink for warm introductions, adopt these techniques

Understand TeamLink:

TeamLink aggregates the LinkedIn connections of your entire sales team.

It identifies shared connections that can be used for warm introductions.

Access TeamLink Connections:

In LinkedIn Sales Navigator, navigate to the "Connections" tab.

Choose "TeamLink Connections" to view the combined network of your sales team.

Identify Shared Connections:

TeamLink will highlight shared connections between you and your team members.

Identify individuals who can facilitate warm introductions to your target audience.

Filter by team Members:

Refine TeamLink connections by filtering based on specific team members.

This allows you to focus on shared connections within a particular colleague's network.

Review Mutual Connections' Profiles:

Before reaching out, review the profiles of shared

connections.

Understand their roles, interests, and how they align with your business goals.

Select Relevant Shared Connections:

Choose shared connections who are relevant to your industry or prospects.

Prioritize those who may have a genuine interest in your offerings.

Craft personalized introduction requests:

When requesting introductions, craft personalized messages.

Explain the purpose of the introduction and highlight shared interests or goals.

Provide Context and Value:

Clearly articulate why the introduction would be valuable.

Offer context on your background, objectives, and how you can mutually benefit.

Team Collaboration:

Collaborate with your sales team to share insights on shared connections.

Discuss potential introductions and coordinate outreach efforts.

Maintain Professionalism:

Ensure that all interactions, including warm introductions, maintain a high level of professionalism.

Respect the time and preferences of both your team members and the introduced connections.

Express Gratitude:

Thank your team members for facilitating warm introductions.

Acknowledge their support in expanding your network.

Follow up with introduced connections:

Once introduced, promptly follow up with the introduced connections.

Continue the conversation and explore opportunities for collaboration.

Feedback and Reporting:

Provide feedback to your team on the outcomes of warm introductions.

Use reporting features to track the success and impact of TeamLink efforts.

Encourage Team Engagement:

Encourage your sales team to actively use and contribute to TeamLink.

The more engaged the team, the more powerful the collective network becomes.

LinkedIn Sales Navigator Mobile App:

Utilize the LinkedIn Sales Navigator mobile app to access TeamLink on the go.

Stay connected and responsive even when away from your desktop.

Iterate and Optimize:

Regularly review and optimize your TeamLink strategy.

Adjust your approach based on the outcomes and evolving business goals.

Educate Team Members:

Provide training and guidance to your sales team on maximizing the benefits of TeamLink.

Share best practices and success stories.

Coordinate outreach Campaigns:

Coordinate outreach campaigns with your team based on shared connections.

Develop a cohesive approach to warm introductions for specific campaigns or initiatives.

Promote cross-team collaboration:

If applicable, encourage collaboration with other teams (e.g., marketing, customer success) to broaden your network further.

Inmail Strategies For Effective Communication

Crafting Compelling InMail Messages

Crafting compelling InMail messages on LinkedIn is crucial for effective communication and successful outreach. InMail provides an opportunity to connect with individuals outside your network and initiate meaningful conversations.

Crafting compelling email messages is an art that combines personalization, clarity, and value proposition. By paying attention to these elements, you can increase the likelihood of engaging your audience and building meaningful connections on LinkedIn.

Adopt these guidelines.

Personalize Your InMail:

Address the recipient by name.

Reference a specific detail from their profile, such as their recent achievements or shared interests.

Start with a strong subject line:

Create a subject line that grabs attention.

Keep it concise and intriguing to encourage the recipient to open the message.

Express genuine interest:

Clearly state why you are reaching out.

Express genuine interest in the recipient's work, achievements, or contributions.

Provide Context:

Explain how you discovered the recipient or what sparked your interest.

Context helps the recipient understand the purpose of your message.

Highlight mutual connections or interests:

If applicable, mention mutual connections or shared interests.

This creates a sense of familiarity and common ground.

Focus on Value:

Clearly articulate the value you bring or how the recipient can benefit.

Tailor your message to highlight the relevance and potential impact.

Be concise and direct.

Keep your message concise and to the point.

Busy professionals appreciate messages that respect their time.

Customize for your audience:

Tailor your message based on the recipient's role, industry, or specific circumstances.

A customized approach demonstrates effort and relevance.

Share a Brief Introduction:

Introduce yourself briefly and mention your role or expertise.

Build credibility by showcasing why you are a valuable connection.

Propose Clear Next Steps:

Clearly outline the next steps or actions you propose.

Whether it's a meeting, a call, or collaboration, make it easy for the recipient to respond.

Highlight Common Goals:

If your goals align, emphasize how collaboration can benefit both parties.

Showcase shared objectives and potential synergies.

Use a friendly tone.

Maintain a professional yet friendly tone.

Avoid sounding too formal; aim for approachability.

Include a Call-to-Action (CTA):

End your message with a clear call-to-action.

Prompt the recipient to respond or take the next step in the engagement.

Proofread Your message:

Ensure your InMail is free of grammatical errors and typos.

A polished message reflects professionalism.

Follow LinkedIn Etiquette:

Respect LinkedIn's guidelines and avoid aggressive or spammy language.

Keep your message in line with professional communication norms.

Test and Iterate:

Experiment with different messaging approaches.

Analyze response rates and iterate based on what works best.

Be Transparent:

If you're reaching out for a specific reason (e.g., job opportunity, collaboration), be transparent about it.

Honesty fosters trust in professional communication.

Utilize Data and Insights:

If you have relevant data or insights to share, incorporate them into your message.

Data-driven communication can add credibility.

Mobile-Friendly Formatting:

Keep in mind that many users check LinkedIn on mobile devices.

Ensure your message is readable and impactful on both desktop and mobile.

Follow Up Appropriately:

If the recipient doesn't respond, consider a polite follow-up.

Avoid being too persistent; respect the recipient's decision.

Best Practices For Inmail Outreach

InMail outreach on LinkedIn requires a thoughtful approach to ensure your messages are well-received and lead to meaningful connections or collaborations.

By following these best practices, you can enhance the effectiveness of your InMail outreach and increase the likelihood of building meaningful connections on LinkedIn. Remember that thoughtful and personalized communication is key to establishing professional relationships.

Here are some best practices for InMail outreach:

Research Your Recipients:

Before sending an InMail, thoroughly research the

individuals you're reaching out to.

Understand their roles, interests, and recent activities to tailor your message.

Personalize Your Messages:

Craft personalized InMail messages for each recipient.

Mention specific details from their profile to show genuine interest.

Start with a Strong Subject Line:

Create a compelling subject line that encourages recipients to open your InMail.

Keep it concise and intriguing.

Express Clear Intentions:

Clearly state why you're reaching out.

Whether it's for networking, collaboration, or a job opportunity, be transparent about your intentions.

Provide Value Upfront:

Communicate the value you offer in the opening lines.

Highlight how the recipient can benefit from the connection.

Be Concise and Direct:

Keep your InMail messages concise and to the point.

Busy professionals appreciate clarity and brevity.

Build a Connection:

Establish a connection by finding common ground or mentioning shared interests.

Foster a sense of familiarity and rapport.

Customize Based on Roles:

Tailor your messages based on the roles and industries of your recipients.

Demonstrate relevance to their professional context.

Use Polite and Professional Language:

Maintain a professional tone throughout your message.

Avoid overly casual or formal language unless it aligns with the recipient's communication style.

Include a Call-to-Action (CTA):

Clearly outline the next steps or actions you propose.

Encourage the recipient to respond or take a specific action.

Acknowledge Shared Connections:

If you have shared connections, acknowledge them in your InMail.

This can create a sense of trust and commonality.

Follow LinkedIn Etiquette:

Adhere to LinkedIn's communication guidelines.

Avoid aggressive language, excessive follow-ups, or unsolicited promotional content.

Proofread Thoroughly:

Ensure your InMail is free of grammatical errors and typos.

A well-written message reflects professionalism.

Test and Iterate:

Experiment with different messaging approaches.

Analyze response rates and adjust your strategy based on

performance.

Respect Recipients' Time:

Acknowledge that professionals have busy schedules.

Clearly communicate the purpose of your message and respect their time.

Use Data and Metrics:

If relevant, incorporate data or metrics that highlight your achievements or success.

Data-driven messages can add credibility.

Follow Up Strategically:

If a recipient doesn't respond, consider a polite and respectful follow-up.

Avoid being overly persistent or pushy.

Optimize for Mobile Viewing:

Ensure your InMail messages are readable and impactful on both desktop and mobile devices.

Many users check LinkedIn on their mobile phones.

Align with Recipient's Goals:

Showcase how your message aligns with the recipient's professional goals.

Make it clear why connecting with you would be beneficial for them.

Maintain a Professional Signature:

Include a professional signature at the end of your InMail.

This adds a personal touch and provides additional contact information.

Managing And Tracking Inmail Conversations

Effectively managing and tracking your InMail conversations on LinkedIn is crucial for maintaining professional relationships, tracking responses, and optimizing your outreach strategy.

By implementing these strategies, you can efficiently manage and track your InMail conversations on LinkedIn, leading to more effective communication and better outcomes in building and nurturing professional connections.

The following are strategies for managing and tracking InMail conversations:

Use LinkedIn Sales Navigator:

Consider using LinkedIn Sales Navigator for enhanced InMail capabilities.

Sales Navigator provides additional features and insights for managing your outreach.

Create a System for Organization:

Develop a system for organizing your InMail conversations.

Use folders, tags, or labels to categorize conversations based on stages, priorities, or topics.

Set Follow-Up Reminders:

Set reminders or calendar events for follow-up actions.

This ensures that you stay on top of your InMail conversations and don't miss important opportunities.

Utilize the "Notes" Feature:

Take advantage of LinkedIn's "Notes" feature within profiles.

Record important details and context about each connection for future reference.

Track Response Rates:

Monitor and track the response rates of your InMail messages.

Analyze which messages are more effective and adjust your strategy accordingly.

Implement a CRM System Integration:

Integrate LinkedIn Sales Navigator with your Customer Relationship Management (CRM) system.

This allows for seamless tracking of InMail conversations within your broader sales process.

Label Important Connections:

Use labels or tags to identify particularly important or high-priority connections.

This can help you prioritize your follow-up and engagement efforts.

Segment Your Outreach:

Segment your InMail outreach based on different criteria.

This could include industry, role, or geographic location, allowing for targeted and personalized messaging.

Evaluate Engagement Metrics:

Evaluate metrics such as open rates, click-through rates, and response rates.

Use these metrics to refine your messaging strategy and content.

Establish a Follow-Up Schedule:

Establish a systematic follow-up schedule for ongoing engagement.

Regular, strategic follow-ups can nurture relationships over time.

Respond Promptly:

Aim to respond promptly to incoming messages.

Timely responses contribute to building a positive and responsive professional image.

Monitor LinkedIn Notifications:

Keep a close eye on LinkedIn notifications for new messages.

This ensures that you stay aware of and promptly respond to incoming communications.

Use Message Templates Wisely:

Develop message templates for efficiency, but use them judiciously.

Personalize each message to maintain a genuine and authentic communication style.

Review Conversation History:

Before reaching out, review your conversation history with

a connection.

This helps you tailor your messages and demonstrate continuity in your communication.

Evaluate Conversion Rates:

Assess the conversion rates from InMail conversations to desired outcomes (e.g., meetings, collaborations).

Use this data to refine your overall outreach strategy.

Optimize Based on Feedback:

Pay attention to feedback received during InMail conversations.

Adjust your approach based on the insights gained from interactions.

Regularly Update Contact Information:

Keep contact information up to date within your CRM or LinkedIn Sales Navigator.

Accurate information ensures effective communication.

Participate in LinkedIn Groups:

Engage in relevant LinkedIn groups to supplement your InMail outreach.

Group interactions can complement and strengthen your outreach efforts.

Consider A/B Testing:

Experiment with A/B testing for different elements in your InMail messages.

Test subject lines, messaging styles, or calls-to-action to identify what resonates best.

Seek Feedback from Colleagues:

Collaborate with colleagues to gather insights on your InMail strategy.

Share experiences and best practices for continuous improvement.

Monitoring And Engaging With Updates

Real-time updates on LinkedIn are a valuable resource for staying informed about the latest activities, achievements, and insights of your connections and the broader professional community. Engaging with real-time updates is crucial for building and maintaining meaningful relationships on the platform.

By actively monitoring and engaging with real-time updates on LinkedIn, you not only stay informed but also contribute to the vibrancy of your professional network. Consistent and genuine interaction with your connections' updates fosters a supportive community and enhances the overall networking experience on the platform.

Here's why real-time updates are important and how to effectively monitor and engage with them:

Importance of Real-Time Updates:

Stay Informed:

Real-time updates provide a live stream of information about your connections, including job changes, work anniversaries, and published content.

Staying informed helps you engage meaningfully and celebrate the achievements of your professional network.

Build Relationships:

Engaging with updates allows you to congratulate connections on their accomplishments and show genuine interest in their professional journey.

Building relationships involves actively participating in the successes and milestones of your network.

Professional Networking:

Real-time updates provide opportunities for organic and timely interactions.

Engaging promptly with updates demonstrates your commitment to maintaining a dynamic and connected professional network.

Content Discovery:

Stay abreast of the content shared by your connections in real-time.

Discovering and engaging with relevant content enhances your industry knowledge and facilitates meaningful discussions.

Networking Opportunities:

Real-time updates often present networking opportunities, such as job changes or new projects.

Being aware of these changes allows you to reach out and

explore potential collaborations or partnerships.

Demonstrate Active Presence:

Regularly engaging with updates showcases your active presence on the platform.

It reinforces your commitment to fostering a vibrant professional community.

How to Monitor and Engage with Real-Time Updates:

LinkedIn Homepage:

Regularly check your LinkedIn homepage for real-time updates from your connections.

Engage with posts by liking, commenting, or sharing to show your support and interest.

Notifications:

Enable notifications for updates from key connections or specific content types.

Notifications help you stay informed and respond promptly to important updates.

Customize Feed Preferences:

Customize your LinkedIn feed preferences to prioritize updates from specific connections or industries.

Tailoring your feed enhances the relevance of the content you encounter.

Set Engagement Goals:

Set goals for daily or weekly engagement with real-time updates.

Allocate dedicated time to interact with posts and maintain a consistent presence.

Use Hashtags and Follow Topics:

Follow relevant hashtags and topics to discover updates aligned with your interests.

Engage in discussions around trending topics to expand your network.

LinkedIn Sales Navigator:

If you have LinkedIn Sales Navigator, leverage its features to monitor updates more efficiently.

Utilize filters to focus on specific criteria, such as job changes or content sharing.

Share Your Updates:

Contribute to the professional community by sharing your own updates.

Engage with connections who interact with your posts to reciprocate and strengthen relationships.

Celebrate Milestones:

Take the opportunity to celebrate work anniversaries, promotions, and other milestones with your connections.

Sending a congratulatory message fosters a positive and supportive network.

Acknowledge Achievements:

When a connection shares a significant achievement, acknowledge it with a thoughtful comment.

Show genuine enthusiasm for their success.

Join LinkedIn Groups:

Participate in LinkedIn groups relevant to your industry.

Engage with updates and discussions within groups to

broaden your network and knowledge.

Set Reminders for Follow-Up:

If you come across opportunities for collaboration or networking in real-time updates, set reminders for follow-up actions.

Act on these opportunities to strengthen your professional relationships.

LinkedIn Mobile App:

Use the LinkedIn mobile app to stay connected on the go.

Engaging with real-time updates becomes more convenient, allowing you to respond promptly.

Strategies For Monitoring Target Accounts

Monitoring and engaging with updates from target accounts on LinkedIn is crucial for successful account-based marketing and sales strategies. By staying informed about the activities and updates of your target accounts, you can tailor your outreach and engagement efforts more effectively.

By combining effective monitoring strategies with thoughtful and strategic engagement, you can build meaningful connections with your target accounts on LinkedIn. Consistent and genuine interactions contribute to building a positive brand image and can lead to valuable business opportunities.

Here are strategies for monitoring and engaging with updates from target accounts:

Monitoring Strategies:

Create Target Account Lists:

Develop lists of your target accounts based on your sales or marketing objectives.

Organize these lists on LinkedIn to streamline monitoring.

Utilize LinkedIn Sales Navigator:

Leverage LinkedIn Sales Navigator for advanced features that facilitate tracking target accounts.

Create custom lists, save leads, and receive real-time updates about your target accounts.

Set Up Saved Searches:

Create saved searches with specific criteria related to your target accounts.

Receive regular notifications and updates based on the parameters you set.

Follow Target Accounts:

Follow the LinkedIn pages of your target accounts.

Updates from these accounts will appear in your feed, providing real-time information.

Use Hashtags and Keywords:

Identify relevant hashtags and keywords associated with your target accounts.

Follow these hashtags and regularly search for the keywords to discover relevant updates.

Enable Notifications:

Turn on notifications for updates from key individuals within your target accounts.

Receive alerts when they post, ensuring you stay informed promptly.

Customize Your Feed:

Tailor your LinkedIn feed to prioritize updates from your target accounts.

Adjust feed preferences to focus on specific content and connections.

Subscribe to LinkedIn Alerts:

Subscribe to LinkedIn Alerts for updates from your target accounts.

Receive email notifications about significant activities, ensuring you don't miss important updates.

Engagement Strategies:

Regularly Engage with Updates:

Actively engage with updates from your target accounts by liking, commenting, or sharing.

Demonstrate your interest in their content and initiatives.

Craft Personalized Messages:

When engaging with updates, consider sending personalized messages to key individuals.

Express your interest in their work and open the door for further conversation.

Celebrate Achievements:

Celebrate milestones and achievements of your target

accounts.

Send congratulatory messages or comments to foster a positive relationship.

Share Relevant Content:

Share your own content that aligns with the interests and objectives of your target accounts.

Position yourself as a valuable resource within their industry.

Participate in Discussions:

Engage in discussions initiated by your target accounts.

Share your insights and contribute to meaningful conversations.

Offer Assistance or Insights:

Monitor for opportunities where you can provide assistance or valuable insights.

Be proactive in offering support or solutions to challenges they may be facing.

Send Connection Requests:

When appropriate, send personalized connection requests to individuals within your target accounts.

Include a brief message explaining your interest in connecting.

Attend Virtual Events Hosted by Target Accounts:

Participate in virtual events or webinars hosted by your target accounts.

Engage with attendees and build connections within the organization.

Use Direct Messages Strategically:

Strategically use direct messages to initiate one-on-one conversations with key decision-makers.

Share relevant information or request a brief meeting.

Monitor Job Changes:

Stay informed about job changes within your target accounts.

Reach out to individuals in new roles to reinforce your relationship.

Coordinate with Sales Team:

Collaborate with your sales team to align engagement efforts with the overall account strategy.

Share insights and coordinate outreach for maximum impact.

Share Case Studies or Success Stories:

Share relevant case studies or success stories with your target accounts.

Demonstrate how your products or services can address their specific needs.

Participate in LinkedIn Groups:

Join LinkedIn groups relevant to your target accounts' industries.

Engage in discussions within these groups to build connections.

Measure and Analyze Engagement:

Regularly analyze your engagement efforts with target accounts.

Evaluate which strategies are most effective and adjust your approach accordingly.

Incorporate a Soft Touch:

Avoid overly promotional or aggressive approaches.

Maintain a soft touch and focus on building relationships gradually.

Engaging With Relevant Content

Engaging with relevant content on LinkedIn is a powerful strategy for building connections, establishing thought leadership, and fostering professional relationships. By actively participating in discussions, sharing insights, and supporting your network, you can enhance your visibility and contribute to a vibrant professional community.

By actively monitoring and engaging with relevant content on LinkedIn, you can build a strong professional network, showcase your expertise, and contribute to meaningful discussions within your industry. Consistent and thoughtful engagement positions you as an active and valuable member of the professional community.

Monitor and engage with relevant content on LinkedIn with these tips:

Monitoring Strategies:

Follow Relevant Hashtags:

Identify and follow industry-specific hashtags relevant to

your interests and expertise.

Stay updated on trending topics within your field.

Curate Your Feed:

Customize your LinkedIn feed to prioritize content from thought leaders, industry influencers, and connections.

Unfollow or mute irrelevant content to streamline your feed.

Use Saved Searches:

Create saved searches based on keywords or topics that align with your professional interests.

Receive notifications for new content matching your criteria.

Subscribe to Newsletters:

Subscribe to newsletters or updates from industry publications and influencers.

Stay informed about the latest news and trends in your field.

Engage in LinkedIn Groups:

Join and actively participate in LinkedIn groups related to your industry.

Monitor group discussions and contribute valuable insights.

Enable Content Notifications:

Turn on notifications for specific individuals or companies whose content you find particularly valuable.

Receive alerts when they share new posts or updates.

Explore LinkedIn Events:

Explore and join LinkedIn Events relevant to your industry or interests.

Engage with event discussions and content.

Engagement Strategies:

Like, Comment, and Share:

Engage with content by liking, commenting, and sharing posts that resonate with you.

Share your thoughts, insights, or relevant experiences in the comments.

Provide Value in Comments:

When commenting, focus on adding value to the discussion.

Share additional insights, ask thoughtful questions, or provide constructive feedback.

Acknowledge and Tag Connections:

Acknowledge your connections by tagging them in relevant content.

This can initiate conversations and strengthen your professional relationships.

Share Personal Experiences:

Share personal experiences related to the content.

Authentic storytelling can resonate with your network and humanize your professional presence.

Create and Share Content:

Contribute to the professional community by creating and

sharing your own content.

Share articles, blog posts, or insights that showcase your expertise.

Participate in Polls and Surveys:

Engage in polls and surveys shared by your connections.

Share your opinions and learn more about the perspectives of others.

Initiate Conversations:

Use engaging content as a conversation starter.

Initiate discussions with your connections based on shared interests or topics.

Utilize Direct Messages Wisely:

Reach out to connections through direct messages to discuss specific content.

Personalize your messages and express your interest in their perspectives.

Collaborate on Content:

Collaborate with others in your network on content creation or joint projects.

This fosters collaboration and expands your reach.

Highlight Key Takeaways:

Share key takeaways from articles or posts you find insightful.

Summarize information for your network to spark interest and discussion.

Follow Thought Leaders:

Identify and follow thought leaders in your industry.

Engage with their content to expand your network and stay updated on industry trends.

Respond to Comments on Your Posts:

Respond promptly to comments on your own posts.

Encourage further discussion and acknowledge the contributions of others.

Express Gratitude:

Express gratitude to connections who engage with your content.

This encourages a positive and supportive professional community.

Share Industry News:

Share relevant industry news and updates.

Position yourself as a source of valuable information within your network.

Participate in Trending Conversations:

Monitor trending topics and join conversations that align with your expertise.

Your participation can enhance your visibility within the professional community.

Attend Virtual Events:

Engage with content shared during virtual events.

Comment on event posts and connect with attendees to broaden your network.

Monitor Analytics:

Use LinkedIn analytics to monitor the performance of your posts.

Evaluate engagement metrics and refine your content strategy accordingly.

Align with Brand Values:

Ensure that your engagement aligns with your personal or brand values.

Maintain a professional and positive online presence.

CONCLUSION

In the vast expanse of digital landscapes and professional connections, our journey through the intricacies of LinkedIn Sales Navigator has been both enlightening and transformative. As we conclude this exploration, we stand at the intersection of possibility and strategy, equipped with the tools to navigate the dynamic realm of sales, marketing, and business growth.

Charting Your Course:

LinkedIn Sales Navigator is not merely a platform; it is a compass guiding professionals toward strategic networking and fruitful connections. It empowers you to chart your course through the ever-shifting landscape of modern business, where success is not just about who you know but how effectively you engage and nurture those connections.

Precision in Connectivity:

The evolution of LinkedIn Sales Navigator has bestowed upon us a set of precise instruments to navigate the complex waters of professional networking. From advanced search filters to AI-driven recommendations, the platform enables a level of precision in connectivity that transcends traditional methods, ensuring that each connection is not just a link but a potential pathway to success.

Adapting to Change:

In the prologue, we acknowledged the imperative of adaptation to technological changes. Now, armed with the insights and strategies presented in this guide, you are not merely an observer of change but an active participant, steering your ship through the winds of technological evolution. LinkedIn Sales Navigator is your ally in this journey of perpetual adaptation.

Strategic Networking Unveiled:

Unveiling the layers of LinkedIn Sales Navigator has been a revelation in strategic networking. It's not just about the numbers of connections but the quality of engagements. From lead recommendations to InMail strategies, the platform offers a spectrum of tools that elevate your networking game, transforming casual interactions into strategic alliances.

A Future-Focused Outlook:

As we gaze into the future, the emerging trends we explored in the epilogue become signposts for our journey ahead. The horizons of social selling, personalization at scale, and the integration of AI are not distant; they are the waypoints that will shape the landscape of LinkedIn Sales Navigator and professional networking in the years to come.

Your Success Story Awaits:

The pages of this guide have unfolded the capabilities of LinkedIn Sales Navigator, but the story is far from over. Your success story with the platform is a narrative waiting to be written, shaped by your insights, engagement strategies, and the meaningful connections you forge. As you implement the knowledge gained, remember that every click, message, and connection is a stroke on the canvas of your success.

In concluding this journey, let the knowledge gleaned from these pages be the wind in your sails as you navigate the expansive sea of opportunities that LinkedIn Sales Navigator presents. Whether you are a seasoned professional seeking to amplify your network or a budding entrepreneur navigating the complexities of business growth, the tools and strategies within this guide are the compass guiding you toward success.

As you embark on the chapters beyond this conclusion, may your endeavors be met with fruitful connections, strategic engagements, and a network that propels you toward your professional aspirations. Here's to your continued success with LinkedIn Sales Navigator—a tool that empowers you not just to connect but to navigate a course towards unparalleled professional achievements.